To Sam our very a
on your baptism d
with all our love,

Nana o Grandad xxxx

Your Baptism

Celebrating
new life

May God pour out blessings
upon you
all the days of your life

Your Baptism

You were loved before you were born.

Pauline
BOOKS & MEDIA

All about you

This is a photograph of you when you were born.

Your birth date is   13th August 2015

You were born at   Homerton Hospital

God says this to you

I have called you by your name;
you are mine.

You are precious in my sight,
and important –
for I have loved you.

Isaiah 43:1,4

About your name

We chose to name you

Samuel   John   Vincent   Clarke

because

Samuel — favourite name

John — after Grandad John + Grandpa Anthony John

Vincent — after your dad's grandad

Your name means

Gift from God

All about our family

Grandad - John Clarke

Nanna - Leslie Clarke

Kate Martin - aunty   Dan Martin - uncle

daddy - Paul Clarke

Grandma Ruth + Grandpa Antony Harding

Auntie Becca + Uncle San Krishnan

Auntie Kirsten + Uncle Alex Beadon

Uncle Nick Harding

mummy - Rachel Clarke

Families are special.

God loves you so much
that he sent his son Jesus

The baptism of Jesus

John began to baptise in the desert;
he preached a baptism of repentance
for the forgiveness of sins.

He preached to the people saying,
"After me comes one who is more powerful than I am;
I have baptised you with water,
but he will baptise you in the Holy Spirit."

Jesus came from Nazareth,
and was baptised by John in the Jordan.
And the moment he came up out of the water,
heaven opened before him
and he saw the Spirit coming down on him like a dove.
And these words were heard from heaven,
"You are my Son, the Beloved, the One I have chosen."

cf Mark 1:4–11

Jesus

was sent by God to teach all of us what God is like.

Because Jesus is God's own son,

in him we see what God is like.

loving

kind

forgiving

gentle

understanding

generous

Jesus

has a special love for children.

He said, "Let the little children come to me."
The Gospel of Matthew chapter 19 verse 14

Our treasures

Jesus

taught us when we pray to ask the Father in his name.

We begin our prayers with

the sign of the cross

In the name of the Father
and of the Son
and of the Holy Spirit.
Amen.

Before you could pray,
we said this prayer for you about our hopes for your future.

We blessed you and traced

the sign of the cross

on your heart.

Our treasures

Our baptism makes us children of God and members of God's family.

Jesus

taught us that God is our Father

and he gave us the perfect prayer:

the Our Father

Our Father

who art in heaven

hallowed be thy name.

Thy kingdom come.

Thy will be done

on earth as it is in heaven.

Give us this day our daily bread

and forgive us our trespasses

as we forgive those who trespass against us.

And lead us not into temptation

but deliver us from evil.

Amen.

Your baptism

A photograph of your baptism

Celebrating your baptism

You were baptised on

in the church of

St Dunstan

The name of the priest or deacon who baptised you is

Fr Simon

We chose Claire Ball, Chris Hale, Uncle Nick + Aunty Kate

as your godparents because we know they all love you + will look out for you

What happened

We brought you to the church and **presented you** for baptism.

We were **welcomed** by the celebrant.

We spoke **your name** out loud and **asked for you to be baptised**.

We **promised** to help you learn and follow God's commands
as Jesus taught us, by loving God and all people.

Your **godparents** promised to help us to do this.

The celebrant **welcomed you** on behalf of the Christian community

and **traced the sign of the cross** on your forehead.

We did the same and so did your godparents.

We **listened** to the Word of God.

The scripture readings were

We prayed to all **the saints** in heaven

including the saint whose name you share.

You were **anointed** for the first time with

the **holy oil of catechumens**.

The celebrant traced the sign of the cross

with the holy oil over your heart

and prayed for God to make you strong.

The celebrant touched the **water** and blessed it.

He called upon God our Father, with Jesus his Son

to send the Holy Spirit upon the water

and make it holy for your baptism.

Because you were too small to speak for yourself,

we, your family, **spoke of our faith** in God.

We **promised** to live **our faith** in God our Father,

in Jesus his Son and in the Holy Spirit.

We **promised** to **teach** you and **show** you how to live

as a child of God, all the days of your life.

The celebrant baptised you

in the name of the Father

and of the Son

and of the Holy Spirit.

You are so special that you were **anointed** again,

this time with the holy, precious **oil of chrism**.

The celebrant poured this sweet smelling oil

on the crown of your head.

We prayed with the priest

that just as **Jesus** was **anointed priest, prophet and king**

so may you grow to be like him in everything you do.

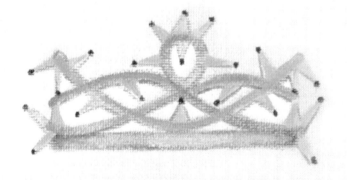

You were clothed in a new **white garment**.

As a newly baptised person,

your white garment is a visible sign

of the dignity of your Christian life.

A **candle** was lit for you from the **Easter candle**

and it was given to you.

We prayed that the light of Jesus remain

in your mind and heart all through your life

until Jesus comes to meet you

and bring you with him to the heavenly kingdom.

The celebrant **blessed your ears and your mouth**.

He placed his hand on them and we prayed with him

that you might hear the Word of God

and be ready to share your faith with others in words and deeds.

The celebrant invited us to pray together

the **Our Father**, the prayer that Jesus taught us,

and that we in turn have taught you.

We, **your first teachers of faith**, received a **special blessing**

so that we keep our promise to help you grow strong in faith

by our word and our example.

Your patron saint

Your patron saint's feast day is celebrated on

About your patron saint

Samuel is an Old Testament prophet

A prayer for you

God our Father, we pray that Samuel

will follow the example of Saint Samuel

and every day see you more clearly, love you more dearly
and follow you more nearly.

Amen.

Your celebration

A message for you

from the priest / deacon

who baptised you.

Your celebration

Nanna + Grandad Clarke

Aunty Kate + Uncle Dan

Claire + Ricky Hoare

Auntie Kirsten, Uncle Alex,

Bella, Noah + Millie Beadon

Veronica — great-aunt

Anna, Louie + Edward Hee

Grandpa + Grandma Harding

Uncle Nick

Auntie Becca, Uncle Sam,

Kai + Anu Krishnan

Your celebration

Photographs

What is next

The celebration of your baptism is the greatest day of your life.
You have begun a wonderful journey
welcomed by the family of God in your parish community.
As we pray and sing together with the community at Sunday Mass
you will grow in the new life you received at baptism.

There are seven sacraments to help you to follow God's call
at all the important stages of your life.

Your journey began with your **Baptism**.

You will receive **Confirmation** and the Holy Spirit
will give you gifts to grow strong in faith and to exercise it in love.

When you receive your first holy **Communion** you will receive
Jesus in the eucharist, to nourish God's life within you.

In **Reconciliation** you will celebrate God's unfailing love
and keep your faith life healthy.

Two sacraments help us live the gift of our baptism
in God's plan for our life, in service to others:
Matrimony celebrates the love and life-long commitment
between husband and wife and to their children.
Holy Orders is for those who have been called by God
to offer service to the community of believers as deacon or priest.

The **Anointing of the Sick** strengthens those who are ill
to serve the whole Church by transforming their suffering
through the love of Jesus.

First published in the United Kingdom in 2012
Pauline Books & Media
Slough SL3 6BS

Text, painting, design MaryLouise Winters fsp

Special thanks to Rev John McLoughlin, Rev Kevin O'Driscoll, Kieran McKeown and Martin Foster

Scripture texts from the *Christian Community Bible*
© 1999 Bernardo Hurault, Claretian Publications, used with permission.

Printed in EEC - AGAM Cuneo (Italy)

ISBN 9781904785644

Pauline
BOOKS & MEDIA
Middle Green, Slough SL3 6BS – UK
+44 (0) 1753 577629
www.pauline-uk.org
email: marketing@pauline-uk.org

Pauline Books & Media is an expression of the ministry of the Daughters of St Paul,
an international Catholic community of religious women, dedicated to spreading the Good News of Jesus Christ.
In imitation of the Apostle Paul, who used every means to proclaim Christ, the sisters work with modern media
and technology for evangelisation.